Kids' First Cookbook

Delicious-Nutritious Treats to Make Yourself!

American Cancer Society®

Published in the United States of America by
The American Cancer Society
HEALTH CONTENT PRODUCTS PUBLISHING GROUP
1599 Clifton Road, NE
Atlanta, Georgia 30329

Library of Congress Cataloging-in-Publication Data
American Cancer Society.
    Kids' first cookbook : delicious-nutritious treats to make yourself! / American Cancer
  Society.-- 1st ed.
      p. cm.
    Summary: A collection of easy-to-make recipes for breakfast foods, snacks, main
dishes, drinks, and desserts.
    ISBN 0-944235-19-0 (alk. paper)
    1. Cookery--Juvenile literature. [1. Cookery.] I. Title.

TX652.5 .A437 1999
641.5'123--dc21

                                        99-052304

Printed in the United States of America.

03   02   01   2   3   4   5

Publisher: Emily Pualwan
Production Manager: Candace Magee
Graphics Specialist: Dana Wagner
Nutritional Analysis: Colleen Doyle, MS, RD and Trisha Vignati, RD

Book design: Shock Design, Inc., Atlanta
Illustration: Nicola Simmonds ("blueprints" and *"3-D Taco"*)
Cover Photograph: Pam Drake
Photography: Billy Howard Photography (pages vii, 16, 19, 20, 27,
28, 33, 48, 49, 50, 54, 64, 65, and 67) and back cover photographs;
Pam Drake (pages 22, 23, 25, 61, 69)

For individual copies, please call 1-888-227-5552
For more information about cancer, call 1-800-ACS-2345

Cooking is one part science,
one part magic,
and two parts fun!

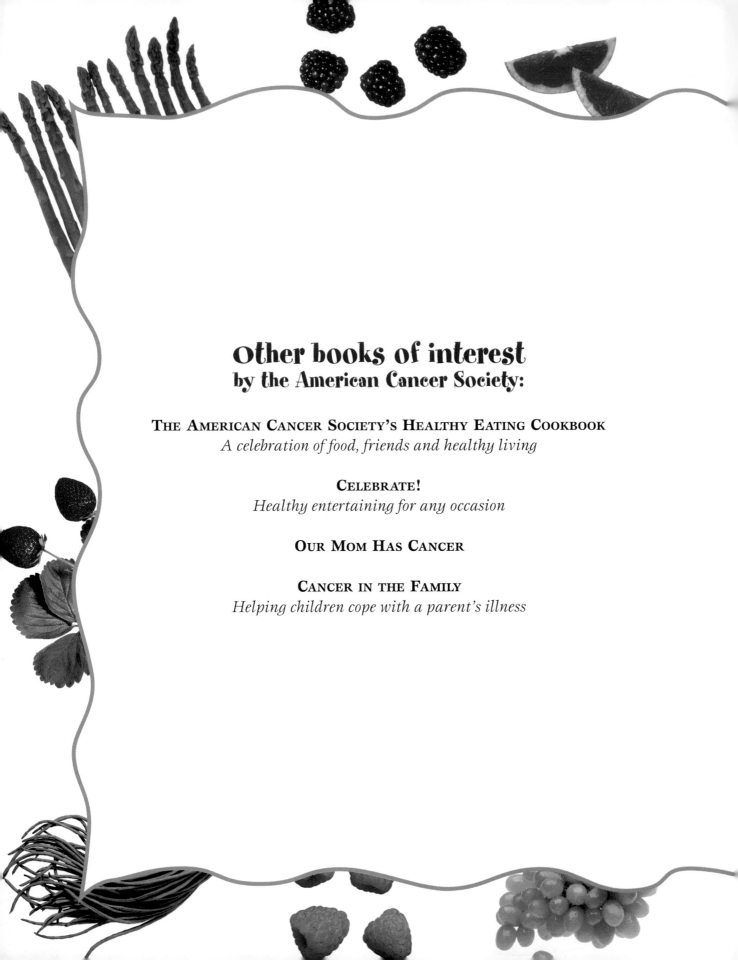

Other books of interest
by the American Cancer Society:

THE AMERICAN CANCER SOCIETY'S HEALTHY EATING COOKBOOK
A celebration of food, friends and healthy living

CELEBRATE!
Healthy entertaining for any occasion

OUR MOM HAS CANCER

CANCER IN THE FAMILY
Helping children cope with a parent's illness

Acknowledgments

We would like to thank all those who have helped us with this project. Thanks to all the kids at Laurel Ridge Elementary School who submitted and tested recipes for us, and to Ms. Frankie Calloway, Principal, who pulled that all together. Thanks to Colleen Doyle, MS, RD and Trish Vignati, RD, who added the science behind the art and gave us nutritional analyses, and to Mr. and Mrs. Richard Blondheim, who most graciously donated their beautiful kitchen for many of the photo shoots. A special thank you to Chef Hilly Blondheim, who donated his time and magic in creation of the foods, and for his enthusiastic work with the kids. And last, but not least, thanks to all our volunteer "kid chefs" — Ali Cullen, Ana Magee, Bobby Newman, Branden Greenberg, George Pualwan and Gracie Magee — who had the most fun of all preparing, cooking, and eating the results!

Contents

Breakfast

Drinks

Snacks

Introduction

Looking for fun and meaningful activities for your kids? Wondering what to make for dinner? Open the pages of the **Kids' First Cookbook** for inspiration and answers.

Inside this unique book are activities, recipes, and cooking tips to help turn meal preparation into an exciting family activity! This fun and enticing book will not only provide you with activities your whole family can share, it will also help your children make healthy and wholesome food choices that will benefit them for a lifetime.

As the nation's foremost authority on cancer and its prevention, the American Cancer Society has published this new cookbook to help kids have fun with good food! And while they're at it, they'll be forming the building blocks for a healthy future. The two leading diseases in this country — heart disease and cancer — are largely lifestyle–related, and the risk of children developing these in their lifetime can be greatly reduced by their eating more fruits, vegetables, and whole grains, eating less fat, and staying active.

It's never too early or too late to begin! Children can learn to make smart food choices early and can carry these choices throughout their life. Parents can also be important role models and help children learn by example. You can do simple things, such as always having bowls of fresh fruit on the counter. Or keep bags of baby carrots and grapes, ready to eat, conveniently located at eye level in the refrigerator.

With the **Kids' First Cookbook,** your children can take charge, don a chef's hat, and create nutritious and delicious snacks and dishes for all meals of the day! From *Creepy Spiders* to *Tornado Swirls,* each recipe explains the tools and ingredients used in preparation, and gives kids step-by-step instructions to create their own masterpieces. *Handy icons* by each recipe identify the level of difficulty. *Secret Tips* give kids an insider's view to cooking techniques, and the *Blueprints* can be great for rainy day activities and school projects. A *Parents' Section* helps mom and dad encourage healthful choices at restaurants, for lunch boxes, and in every day meals.

Give children the most precious gift of all — the gift of good health. Start them on the road to healthy cooking today, and let them create a little magic in your kitchen!

10 Steps to a Healthy You!

1. A Balancing Act

Foods aren't 'good' or 'bad.' It's all about how much and how often you eat them. Use the Food Guide Pyramid on page 10 to help you make your choices. Eating healthy foods will help keep your body strong and will help you do better at school *and* sports.

And don't forget **5 A Day – Every Day!** Fruits and vegetables contain vitamins to help your body be its best. Try to fit in at least five servings each day.

Example of serving sizes:
A banana equals one serving of fruit. So does a handful of baby carrots. A big glass of orange juice equals two servings. See how easy this is?!

2. Feed that Body

Foods are not just tasty to your mouth — they're feeding all parts of your body! When you eat, your body breaks up the food into tiny pieces it uses to make energy. This is called digestion. As a matter of fact, your body will be working on that lunch for about 24 hours! The good things are absorbed by your body, just like a sponge.

Esophagus (food pipe)

Stomach

Small intestine

Large intestine

3. Those Pearly Whites

When you eat, little pieces of food get stuck in your teeth. If the food stays there too long it can rot your teeth. Be sure to brush and floss after meals to keep your teeth looking their best!

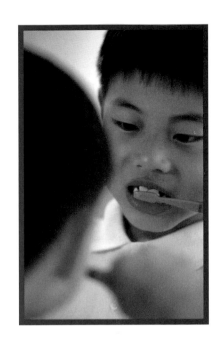

4. Work Those Muscles

There are more than 600 muscles in your body, all working together for a stronger you. Keep those muscles healthy by working up a sweat with biking, hiking, or sports at school. Try to do something every day with your friends and family to keep your body in shape.

5. Water Works

Did you know your body is made up of mostly water? Without water you wouldn't be able to survive. So be sure to drink plenty throughout the day, especially if you're out in the sun or playing hard.

6. Fun in the Sun

When you're out in the sun, remember your skin. Without protection, the sun can give you painful sunburns or blisters. Or make you look old and wrinkled before your time. Just remember **SLIP! SLOP! SLAP!**™ to be safe and have fun in the sun every day!

SLIP on a shirt,

SLOP on sunscreen (with an SPF of 15 or higher),

and SLAP on a hat.

WRAP on sunglasses to protect your eyes.

Hot Tip!

When you are outside and your shadow is shorter than you are, the ultraviolet rays (UV rays) from the sun are *very strong*. You need to protect your skin and eyes.

7. Getting Your ZZZZs

While sleeping may not be your favorite thing to do, it's just as important to your body as good food and physical activity. While you sleep, your body grows and repairs itself, preparing you for the next exciting day.

8. Smoke-Free Air

Always keep the air in your lungs smoke-free. Cigarettes are addicting and can cause all kinds of harm to your body, including a greater risk for heart disease and cancer. Strong, healthy lungs will help you breathe deep and win that race!

9. Saying NO

Keeping your body strong means keeping the bad things out. **ALWAYS SAY NO** to drugs, alcohol or anything else that may harm your body.

10. Do the Check-Up

Remember those yearly visits to the doctor, dentist, and eye doctor? Your doctors help keep you healthy and can spot small problems before they can turn into big ones. Your doctor's office is also a great place to learn about your body and the incredible things it can do.

Kitchen Safety Tips

1. **If you have long hair, tie it back** before you start cooking. Always roll up your shirt sleeves before working in the kitchen.

2. **Always wash your hands** before you get started and after you handle foods. Also wash after touching your hair or rubbing your face, and after handling uncooked meats.

3. **If you need to stand on a step-stool, be sure it's on a flat surface** and has rubber pads to grip the floor.

4. **Always put raw meats on their own plate.** Never put raw meats on the same plate as your other foods.

5. **Make sure paper towels, dish towels and pot holders are away from the stovetop** or anywhere they could catch fire.

6. **Be careful with anything hot.** Use a pot holder that is well padded and dry.

7. **Be sure to have an adult** put things in and take things out of the oven.

HOT

8. **Open pot lids away from you** so you don't get burned by steam.

9. **Never add water to a dish that has hot oil in it.** The oil could splatter and burn.

10. **Keep pot handles pointed toward the back of the stove** so you don't knock into them.

11. **Keep a fire extinguisher in the kitchen** and know how to use it.

12. **Keep all electrical appliances away from water** and keep your hands — especially <u>wet</u> hands! — away from electrical sockets.

13. **Have an adult cut foods** that need to be cut with sharp knives.

14. **Never put sharp knives** or other sharp items into a full sink.

15. **Let hot pots and pans cool** down before you try to clean them.

16. **Make sure the oven and all other appliances are turned off** before leaving the kitchen.

17. **Clean up!!**

Tools of the Trade

spatula

grater

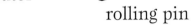
rolling pin

whisk

blender

food processor

hand-held mixer

mixer

pasta maker

toaster

toaster oven

microwave

waffle iron

casserole dish

muffin pan

sauce pan

strainer (colander)

grill

stove

fire extinguisher

How Much Do I Put In?

3 teaspoons = 1 tablespoon

4 tablespoons = ¼ cup

1 cup

2 cups = 1 pint

4 cups = 1 quart

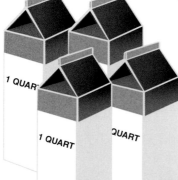 

4 quarts = 1 gallon

How to Read A Food Label

These labels are on the backs and sides of most boxes
and containers of foods you eat.
Do you know what the numbers mean?
Use our guide below to figure it out!

Look for this food label heading on your food packages.

These listings
show the average
serving size
and number of
servings found in
the package.

Both total and
saturated fat are
listed. Too much
saturated fat in
your diet can raise
cholesterol and
bring on heart
disease. You
shouldn't go
above 100% daily
value on either
fats, cholesterol,
or sodium with
what you eat
in a day.

Nutrition Facts

Serving Size 24 pieces (30g)
Servings Per Container About 9

Amount Per Serving
Calories 130   Calories from Fat 40

	% Daily Value*
Total Fat 4.5g	**7%**
Saturated Fat 1g	**4%**
Cholesterol 0mg	**0%**
Sodium 135mg	**6%**
Total Carbohydrate 23g	**8%**
Dietary Fiber Less than 1g	**3%**
Sugars 8g	
Protein 2g	

Vitamin A 0%	•	Vitamin C 0%
Calcium 0%	•	Iron 4%

* Percent Daily Values are based on a 2,000
calorie diet. Your daily values may be higher
or lower depending on your calorie needs:

	Calories	2,000	2,500
Total Fat	Less than	65g	80g
Sat Fat	Less than	20g	25g
Cholesterol	Less than	300mg	300mg
Sodium	Less than	2,400mg	2,400mg
Total Carbohydrate		300g	375g
Dietary Fiber		25g	30g

Tip:
For every 100 calories
in a serving, choose
foods with 3 grams of
fat or less — this is a
lowfat food. So, if
one serving has 200
calories, it can have
6 grams of fat and
still be low fat.

The % value
shows how the
content of this food
compares and fits into
an average 2,000 calo-
rie daily diet. A good
rule of thumb — if a
% daily value is less
than 10, the food
you're looking at is
low in that nutrient.

Food Guide Pyramid for Young Children
A Daily Guide for 2- to 6-Year-Olds

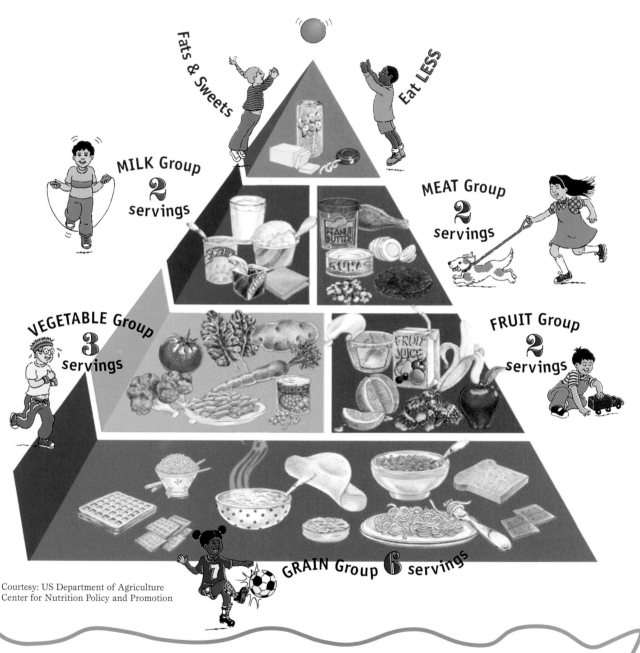

Fats & Sweets — Eat LESS

MILK Group 2 servings

MEAT Group 2 servings

VEGETABLE Group 3 servings

FRUIT Group 2 servings

GRAIN Group 6 servings

Courtesy: US Department of Agriculture
Center for Nutrition Policy and Promotion

The food guide pyramid shows you how to make food choices for a healthy diet. The pyramid divides foods into five major food groups: grains, vegetables, fruits, milk and meat. The small tip of the pyramid shows fats and sweets.

10

Pyramid Basics

The small tip shows that it is best to eat less of foods that contain a lot of fat and sugars. These foods contain calories but few vitamins and minerals.

The **milk group** foods are important for calcium. Two- to 6-year-old children need a total of two servings from the milk group each day.

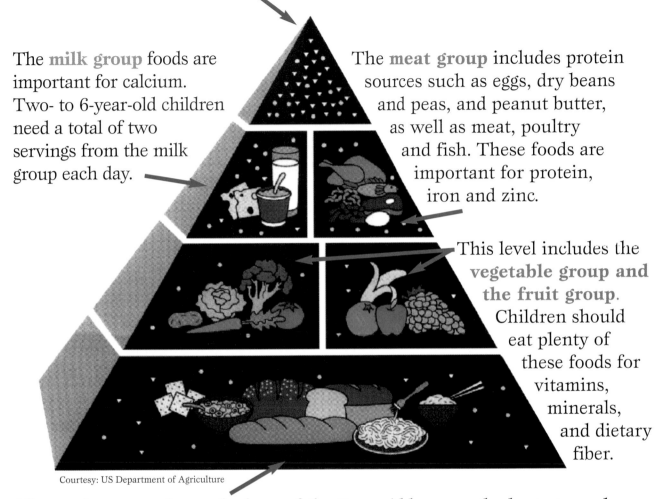

The **meat group** includes protein sources such as eggs, dry beans and peas, and peanut butter, as well as meat, poultry and fish. These foods are important for protein, iron and zinc.

This level includes the **vegetable group and the fruit group**. Children should eat plenty of these foods for vitamins, minerals, and dietary fiber.

Courtesy: US Department of Agriculture

The **grain group** forms the base of the Pyramid because the largest number of servings needed each day comes from this food group. Grain products are important for vitamins, minerals, complex carbohydrates, and dietary fiber.

Be creative! At the store, pick out foods from each of these groups. Choose a new fruit or vegetable each week. At home you can put your choices together and help make dinner, or a snack!

Create a 3-D Taco Pyramid You Can Eat!

In the recipe below you'll be able to make a tasty meal that uses all of the food groups you learned about on the previous pages.

Tasty Taco Pyramid

4 large soft flour tortillas
$\frac{1}{4}$ cup taco sauce
1 15-ounce can pinto beans, drained
$\frac{1}{2}$ cup shredded reduced-fat
　　cheddar cheese

1 cup shredded lettuce
1 cup chopped tomatoes
$\frac{1}{4}$ cup lowfat sour cream (optional)

In a small bowl, mash the beans and mix with the taco sauce.
Now build your pyramid! (Makes four pyramids.)

Take each flour tortilla and place flat on a plate.

Spread the bean mixture over the tortillas.

Sprinkle lettuce and tomatoes.

Next, top with shredded cheese.

Add a small spoonful of the sour cream on top if you choose. And now you're ready to eat your pyramid!

dollop of sour cream

shredded cheese

lettuce

tomatoes

beans

tortilla

Glossary of Cooking Terms

bake – to cook in the oven.

beat – to mix ingredients together with a fork, spoon or a mixer at a high speed. This adds air to the mixture and makes it smooth.

blend – to mix two or more ingredients together with a spoon or a mixer.

boil – to heat liquid in a pan on a stove until big bubbles form. (212° [degrees] Fahrenheit or 100° [degrees] Celsius for water).

broil – to bake at a high temperature in the oven under the broiler. This helps foods turn brown on the top.

calorie – a measure of energy in food.

carbohydrate – a group of nutrients that includes sugar, starch and fiber.

Celsius – a temperature scale measured in degrees (°) where 0 is the freezing point and 100 is the boiling point of water. Abbreviated as **C**.

chill – to place foods in the refrigerator to make them cold.

cholesterol – a fat-like nutrient made in the body and found in every cell.

chop – to cut into small rough shaped pieces on a cutting board.

cool – to let food stand at room temperature until no longer warm. Food can be put on a wire cooling rack to help it cool more evenly.

cream – to mix butter or margarine with sugar in a bowl with a spoon until it becomes creamy.

cube – to cut foods into smaller square pieces using a knife.

dash – a small amount of an ingredient. To add a dash, shake one drop or sprinkle out of a shaker.

dice – to cut into cubes of the same small size.

dissolve – to stir a dry ingredient into a small amount of liquid until it disappears.

dollop – a small serving.

dot – to drop bits of an ingredient randomly over food.

dough – a mixture of flour and water that is thick enough to roll, knead or drop from a spoon.

drain – to pour off liquid from foods by putting food into a strainer or colander to separate the solid from the liquid.

drizzle – to pour lightly from a spoon over a food.

dust – to sprinkle very lightly with flour or sugar on the top of a food.

Fahrenheit – a temperature scale where 32 (degrees) is the freezing point and 212 is the boiling point of water. Abbreviated as **F**.

fat – a nutrient that supplies energy and calories but little else.

fiber – a variety of substances found in plant foods that cannot be fully digested by the body.

flour – to dust greased pans with flour until covered lightly on bottom and sides. Shake out excess flour.

fold – to mix ingredients together using a gentle up and down motion with a spoon.

grate – to rub a food across a grater's tiny punched holes to make small pieces of food.

grease – to cover pans with oil or non-stick vegetable cooking spray before food is put in, to prevent sticking.

grind – to cut or crush in a food grinder.

knead – to mix dough into a smooth mixture by pressing and folding with your hands until soft and smooth.

measure – to use measuring cups or spoons to get the right amount needed for a recipe.

melt – to turn a solid into a liquid by heating it.

mince – to chop very finely.

mix – to combine all ingredients so they are all evenly blended.

nutrition – the science that explores the food you eat and how your body uses it.

peel – to remove the outer skin from a fruit or vegetable with a knife.

protein – a nutrient that is needed for your body to grow and be healthy.

roast – to cook in the oven using dry heat.

roll out – to flatten and spread with a rolling pin.

sauté – to cook quickly in a pan over medium-high heat with a small amount of fat or liquid.

shred – to rub a large food across a surface with medium to large holes or slits to make small pieces.

sift – to put a dry mixture through a sifter to break up the lumps for even measurement.

simmer – to cook in a liquid that is just below boiling, on low heat so small bubbles form.

slice – to cut food into thin pieces with a knife.

sodium – a mineral found in salt which is needed by your body.

stir – to mix round and round with a spoon.

stir–fry – to cook quickly over high heat in a small amount of fat or liquid, using a light tossing motion.

toss – to mix several foods together lightly.

whip – to beat rapidly, usually with a wire whip, to add air.

whisk – to beat ingredients together with a wire whip until they are well blended.

Let's have some FUN in the kitchen!

Recipes

Look for this sign after each recipe name.
It will tell you the recipe's level of difficulty.

NO SWEAT   **MEDIUM**   **MASTER CHEF**

French Toast Fingers

1 egg
1 tablespoon low-fat milk
2 slices whole wheat bread
cooking spray
powdered sugar and
    cinnamon for topping

Preheat oven to 350 degrees F.
Spray a sheet pan with cooking spray and set aside.

Cut each slice of bread into four strips, lengthwise. You'll have eight strips in all.

In a small bowl, combine egg and milk and beat with a fork until frothy. Dip each strip of bread in the egg mixture and coat completely. Lay the strips on the cooking sheet. When all strips have been dipped and laid on the sheet pan, place in oven and bake for about 12 minutes until brown.

Sprinkle lightly with powdered sugar and cinnamon and serve!

Makes 2 servings. 123 calories, 4 fat grams per serving.

Easy Monkey Bread

1 tube of quick biscuits (6 count)
¼ cup cinnamon sugar
   cooking spray
   bundt pan (ring-shaped pan that
      has a tube in the center)

Preheat oven to 400 degrees F. Coat bundt pan thoroughly with cooking spray.

Cut each biscuit into four pieces. Roll each piece of biscuit into a ball.

Roll in cinnamon sugar mixture until covered.

Drop pieces around the sprayed bundt pan. Bake in oven for about 10 minutes, or until the biscuits are done and brown on top. Flip the bread out of the pan and pull apart to serve.

Makes 6 servings. 72 calories, 3 fat grams per serving.

Pizza for Breakfast!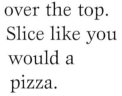

2 eggs
½ cup chopped tomatoes
4 tablespoons low-fat mozzarella cheese
cooking spray

In a small bowl, beat the eggs with a fork until smooth. Preheat a small non-stick skillet on high and coat lightly with cooking spray. Lower the heat to medium-high and pour in eggs. Cook until eggs are solid.

Slide your Breakfast "Pizza" onto a plate. Add cheese and tomatoes evenly over the top. Slice like you would a pizza.

From George P., age 6

Makes 2 servings. 128 calories, 7 fat grams per serving.

Tacos for Breakfast!

4 small flour tortillas
4 eggs
4 slices of turkey bacon, cooked
½ cup low-fat cheddar cheese, shredded

In a microwave-safe bowl, mix eggs and cheese together and cover with a paper towel. Microwave on high for 2-3 minutes, stirring once after 1 minute, until fluffy.

Heat tortillas for a few seconds in the microwave, then fill with egg and cheese mixture. Top with bacon slice, fold and eat.

Secret Tip!

Be sure to use a big enough bowl when you microwave eggs. They'll rise up to more than **TWICE** their size!

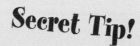

Makes 4 servings. 223 calories, 11 fat grams per serving.

Raspberry Slush

3 cups frozen raspberries, slightly thawed
1 teaspoon vanilla extract
1 cup non-fat plain yogurt
2 tablespoons sugar

Mix all ingredients together until smooth, and serve.

Makes 2 servings. 407 calories, 2 fat grams per serving.

Super Duper Fruity Smoothie

1 cup orange juice
1 cup fresh pineapple, cut into 1-inch chunks
5 fresh strawberries or blueberries
1 cup banana, cut into ¼-inch thick disks
1 tablespoon honey
1 cup ice

Set aside a few pieces of cut fruit for garnish.

Combine orange juice, pineapple, banana, honey and ice cubes in a blender. Blend, crush, puree until smooth.
   (Try all the buttons — it's fun!)

Garnish with strawberry and pineapple and serve.

From Rylan B., age 8

Makes 4 servings. 103 calories, less than 1 fat gram per serving.

Pineapple Orange Slushie

2 cups canned crushed pineapple in unsweetened juice,
lightly drained
½ cup evaporated skim milk
¼ cup orange juice concentrate
10 ice cubes

Combine pineapple, milk and
orange juice in a blender and blend
until smooth.

Add ice cubes, one at a time
until thick and smooth.

Makes 2 servings. 292 calories, less than 1 fat gram per serving.

Berry Banana Shake-up

4 scoops low-fat vanilla frozen yogurt
10 fresh strawberries, cleaned
½ banana

Combine all ingredients in a blender and blend until smooth. Pour into a cup and enjoy!

From Peter T., age 6

Makes 2 servings. 159 calories, 2 fat grams per serving.

Pineapple-Banana Milk Shake

1 cup canned crushed pineapple,
    packed in juice
1 medium banana, cut up
1 cup ice water
$\frac{2}{3}$ cup non-fat dry milk powder
8 ice cubes

Combine pineapple, banana, water and milk powder in a blender and blend until smooth. Add ice cubes, two at a time, and continue to blend until thick and smooth.

Makes 2 servings. 208 calories, less than 1 fat gram per serving.

Witches' Brew

16 fluid ounces of real fruit punch (no sugar added)
4 cups seltzer water
8 scoops low-fat frozen vanilla yogurt

Pour 4 ounces of fruit juice into glass and add two scoops of frozen vanilla yogurt. Pour in one cup of seltzer water and stir.

Drink immediately or it will bubble over!

Makes 4 servings. 179 calories, 2 fat grams per serving.

Creepy Spiders

2 Ritz® crackers
1 tablespoon reduced-fat peanut butter
8 small pretzel sticks
2 raisins

To make a spider, put a small spoonful of peanut butter on a cracker and make a sandwich with another cracker. Stick four pretzel sticks in each side for the legs. Stick two raisin "eyes" on top with a bit of peanut butter.

Spook the sitter!

Makes 1 serving. 146 calories, 7 fat grams per serving.

Monster Mouths

3 apples, cored and sliced into 8 pieces, skins on
3 cups reduced-fat creamy peanut butter
1 cup miniature marshmallows
1 cup raisins
3 fruit roll-ups

Spread peanut butter on apple slices. Decorate with marshmallows for teeth and raisins for rotten teeth. Add fruit roll-up slices for tongues.

From Matthew S., age 5

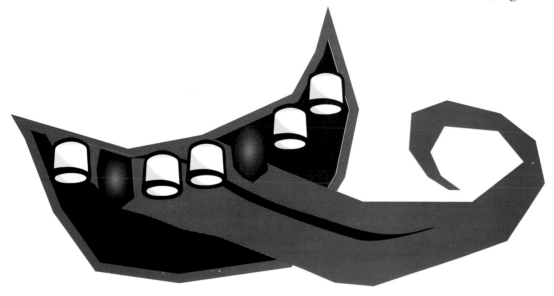

Makes 8 servings. 300 calories, 12 fat grams per serving.

IFOs (Identified Fruit Objects)

1 orange, cut in half crosswise
2 cups small or cut-up fruit pieces (such as grapes, strawberries, melon balls, banana chunks, pineapple chunks)

wooden skewers or toothpicks

Place orange half, cut-side down, on serving plate. Thread fruit pieces alternatively onto wooden skewers and insert randomly into orange half.

From Kaitlyn S., age 6

Makes 4 servings. 77 calories, less than 1 fat gram per serving.

Pogo Sticks

1 banana, sliced thick
1 pear, peeled and cut in 1-inch cubes
1 apple, peeled and cut in 1-inch cubes
1 cup low-fat cereal (crushed granola types work best)
1 cup reduced-fat frozen whipped topping
1 package pretzel sticks (18 thin pretzels)

Put a pretzel stick in each piece of fruit and dip in cool whip. Shake off excess cool whip, coat with cereal, and eat!

From Trey B., age 7

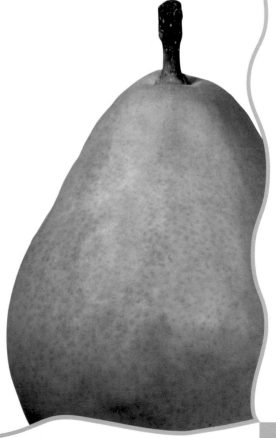

Fuzzy Caterpillars

2 bananas
¼ cup shredded coconut
¼ cup reduced-fat peanut butter
8 raisins

Peel bananas and cut off the ends. Spread
peanut butter over the entire banana and roll in the
coconut. Cut in half to make four caterpillars. Add two raisin
"eyes" to each caterpillar.

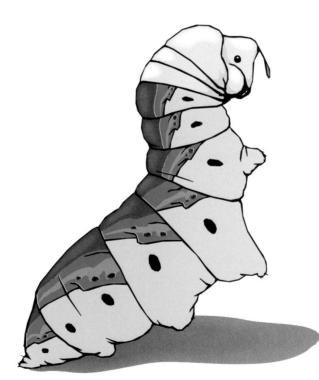

Makes 4 servings. 182 calories, 8 fat grams per serving.

Go Fish

1 cup low-fat cream cheese or Neufchatel cheese
4 tablespoons plain low-fat yogurt
blue food coloring
little fish crackers
pretzel sticks

In a small bowl blend together the cream cheese and yogurt until smooth. Add just a few drops of blue food coloring and mix until all blue.

Pour mixture into a wide soup dish or shallow bowl and place goldfish all around.

Use pretzel sticks as fishing poles and dip out your fish.

Makes 4 servings. 224 calories, 12 fat grams per serving.

Bugs on a Log

4 stalks of celery, cleaned but with some leaves left on
½ cup low-fat cream cheese or
Neufchatel cheese
currants, raisins, and shelled sunflower seeds

Cut the cleaned celery stalks into four-inch logs. Fill each log with a tablespoon of cream cheese. Put a few currants, raisins and sunflower seeds on top for your bugs.

Makes 8 servings. 81 calories, 3 fat grams per serving.

Carrots on the Ranch

bag of baby carrots
$\frac{1}{4}$ cup fat-free sour cream
$\frac{1}{4}$ cup low-fat ranch dressing
pepper to taste

In a small bowl mix together the sour cream and the ranch dressing. Add pepper to taste. Take the baby carrots and dip in dressing to eat.

Makes 4 servings. 141 calories, 4 fat grams per serving.

35

Taco Layer Dip

1 16-ounce container fat-free sour cream
1 envelope taco seasoning
1 head lettuce, shredded
2 tomatoes, chopped
1 cup low-fat shredded cheddar cheese
1 package low-fat tortilla chips

Combine sour cream and taco seasoning in a small bowl and chill for one hour.

Take a large shallow dish and layer the ingredients, one by one, in the dish in the following order: sour cream mix, lettuce, tomatoes, cheese. Serve with tortilla chips for dipping.

Makes 8 servings. 198 calories, 6 fat grams per serving.

Bugs at the Beach

4 honey graham crackers (8 squares), crushed
1 small box of raisins
2 tablespoons of chocolate sprinkles

Secret Tip!

Place graham crackers in a plastic zip-lock bag and crush with a rolling pin or soft mallet.

Spread the graham cracker crumbs on two plates. Sprinkle raisins (slug bugs) and chocolate sprinkles (ants) over the crumbs and eat with your fingers!

Makes 2 servings. 230 calories, 3 fat grams per serving.

Peanut Butter Banana Sandwich

2 tablespoons reduced-fat peanut butter
1 small banana, peeled and sliced
4 slices raisin bread

Spread peanut butter on two slices of bread. Arrange banana slices on top and cover with remaining bread. Cut into quarters and serve.

Makes 2 servings. 290 calories, 9 fat grams per serving.

Peanut Butter and Jelly Roundups

4 teaspoons reduced-fat creamy peanut butter
2 teaspoons grape jelly
8 Ritz® crackers

In a small bowl mix some peanut butter and jelly together until smooth. Spread onto a Ritz® cracker and top with another cracker to make sandwiches.

From Morgan S., age 6

Makes 2 servings. 108 calories, 5 fat grams per serving.

Yummy Veggie Pizza

1 pre-cooked 14" pizza crust
1 cup pizza sauce
1 cup broccoli, chopped
1 cup mushrooms, sliced
½ cup green pepper, sliced
1 cup low-fat shredded mozzarella cheese

Preheat oven to 400 degrees F.

Spread the pizza sauce on the crust and add broccoli, mushrooms and peppers. Sprinkle cheese on top and bake for about 12 minutes, or until cheese is bubbly and lightly browned.

Remember to let pizza cool for 5 minutes before slicing!

Makes 8 servings. 150 calories, 3 fat grams per serving.

Homemade Pizza Crust

1½ cups all-purpose flour
1½ cups bread flour
½ teaspoon salt

2 cups water <u>plus</u> another ¼ cup very warm *(but <u>not</u> hot!)* water
1 packet fast-rising active dry yeast
1 teaspoon sugar

Preheat oven to 400 degrees F.

Put ¼ cup of warm water into a small bowl. Stir in the sugar and yeast. Let sit for 5 minutes. It will become all bubbly.

Place the flours and salt in food processor or mixer. Stir together at a slow speed for about a minute. Stop the machine and pour in the yeast mixture plus 1¼ cups of the extra water. Slowly mix until a sticky dough starts to form. Add more water, ¼ cup at a time, and mix about 7 minutes on medium speed until the dough becomes smooth and elastic. (If it gets too sticky again, add a little more flour.)

Sprinkle a small handful of flour on rolling pin and cutting board. Place the dough on the board and begin rolling from the middle out to the edges, until it is about ¼" thick. Transfer dough to a baking sheet.

Add your favorite toppings and bake for about 10 minutes.

From Ana M., age 9

Use your imagination to make fun shapes!

French Pizza

1 loaf French bread
2 cups pizza sauce
1 cup low-fat mozzarella cheese, shredded
1 cup canned sliced mushrooms, drained (optional)

Preheat the oven to 375 degrees F.

Cut the bread in half lengthwise. Spread the pizza sauce over both slices and sprinkle with mushrooms and then cheese. Place the pizza on a baking sheet and bake for about 15 minutes, or until the top is brown and bubbly.

Makes 4 servings. 343 calories, 8 fat grams per serving.

Mini Pizzas

2 English muffins, split
½ cup pizza sauce
¼ cup shredded low-fat mozzarella cheese

Toast the English muffins in the toaster until just brown. Spread pizza sauce on each muffin slice and sprinkle with cheese. Toast the pizzas under the broiler in the toaster oven to melt cheese.

From Matthew M., age 5

Pizza on a Stick

1 tube of uncooked bread sticks
1/4 cup low-fat shredded mozzarella cheese
2 tablespoons parmesan cheese
1 cup pizza sauce

Roll out bread sticks (dough) and sprinkle with mozzarella and parmesan cheese. Bake in oven according to package directions, making sure not to burn the cheese.

Microwave the pizza sauce in a microwave-safe bowl for 1-2 minutes until hot. Serve the bread sticks with the pizza sauce as dip.

Makes 8 servings. 129 calories, 3 fat grams per serving.

Build A Bagel Face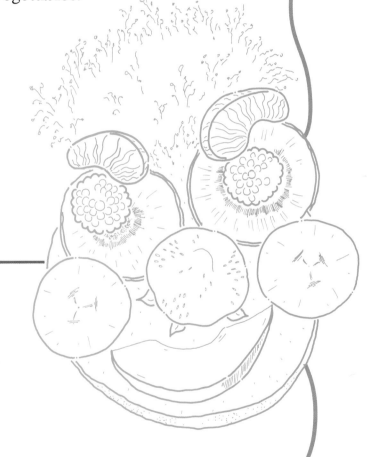

Half of a bagel
low fat cream cheese or Neufchatel cheese

An assortment of the following vegetables:
carrot circles
cucumber half-slices
cherry tomatoes
red peppers, sliced thin
green peppers, sliced thin
black pitted olives
green pitted olives
alfalfa sprouts
bean sprouts
celery slices

Take your bagel and spread
thinly with cream cheese. Then
take the vegetables and have fun
making funny faces you can eat!

Makes 1 serving. 193 calories, 6 fat grams per serving.

Fun Spaghetti and Meatballs Easy as ABC!

1 pound spaghetti (or any shape pasta you like)
2 pounds ground turkey breast
4 cloves garlic, chopped
1 onion, finely chopped
½ cup parmesan cheese
salt and pepper to taste
6 cups spaghetti sauce

alphabet cookie cutters

Secret Tip!

To see if the spaghetti is ready, toss a strand against a wall—*really!* If it sticks to the wall, it's done! If the spaghetti bounces off the wall, it means it's still too hard to chew and needs a few more minutes of cooking.
BUT BE SURE to ask Mom or Dad first, and don't try this on wallpaper!

Preheat oven to 350 degrees F.

Cook the spaghetti according to box directions. Mix the next 5 ingredients together in a mixing bowl. Line a cookie sheet (sheet pan) with foil. Spread meat mixture evenly onto the sheet pan and bake for 15-20 minutes.
When the pasta is done, drain it in your colander (strainer).

Makes 8-10 servings. 449 calories, 10 fat grams per serving.

Remove pan from oven and let it cool a little before you handle the cooked meat. Cut out letter-shaped meatballs with your alphabet cookie cutters.

To serve, put the spaghetti on a plate with some sauce and the meatball shapes and enjoy the compliments!

From Chef Hilly

Sweet Roasted Garlic

1 head of garlic
2 teaspoons olive oil

Preheat oven to 350 degrees F.

Rub the whole head of garlic with olive oil. Wrap completely in foil. Bake in an oven for 1 hour. Remove from oven and cut through the middle, and squeeze out the garlic. Spread on toast or bread.

From Chef Hilly

Makes 2 servings. 18 calories, 1 fat gram per serving.

Super Giant Sea Snails

1½ cups broccoli florets
1 8-ounce package part-skim ricotta cheese
1 egg
1 16-ounce package jumbo pasta shells, cooked
    (you'll want 12 unbroken ones for your recipe)
1 cup pasta sauce

Preheat oven to 350 degrees F.

Cover bottom of casserole dish with ⅓ cup pasta sauce. Bring water to a boil and drop broccoli into the boiling water. Cook until tender; drain. When cool, cut the broccoli into little pieces.

Combine chopped broccoli, ricotta cheese, egg and rest of pasta sauce in a bowl and mix well.

Makes 4 servings. 224 calories, 7 fat grams per serving.

Stuff the mixture into each shell and arrange in a baking dish. Cover with foil and bake for 30 minutes.

Dinner is served!

Groundhogs

1 pound ground turkey breast

1 cup cooked rice (boil-in-bag type is quick and easy)

1 small onion, finely chopped

1 cup bread crumbs

¼ cup ketchup

salt and pepper to taste

¼ cup water

Preheat oven to 350 degrees F.

In a bowl combine turkey breast, cooked rice, chopped onion, bread crumbs and ketchup; mix well. Form small oval-shaped patties and place on baking sheet. Sprinkle with salt and pepper, and add water to bottom of pan. Bake for one hour.

Makes 8 servings. 111 calories, 1 fat gram per serving.

Hawaiian Broccoli

4 cups broccoli florets
2 tablespoons reduced-fat crunchy peanut butter
1 tablespoon soy sauce
1 tablespoon orange juice

Boil broccoli until just cooked. Drain and set aside. Mix all other ingredients together and pour over the top of the broccoli. Serve immediately.

Makes 8 servings. 38 calories, 2 fat grams per serving.

Warm Cinnamon Apples

Two firm green apples (like Granny Smiths), peeled and sliced
2 teaspoons cinnamon sugar

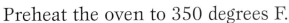

Preheat the oven to 350 degrees F.

Place the sliced apples on a cookie sheet and sprinkle cinnamon sugar over the tops of the slices. Bake in the oven for 15 minutes. Have a grown-up remove from oven. Serve warm.

Makes 2 servings. 96 calories, less than 1 fat gram per serving.

Chicken Swords

4 bamboo skewers

1 pound skinless, boneless chicken breasts, cooked and
   cut in large cubes

1 tablespoon Dijon mustard

¼ cup peach preserves

1 teaspoon lemon juice

Secret Tip!

Soak skewers in water for about 30 minutes before using them so they don't burn when you put them on the grill.

Put chicken cubes in a bowl.

Combine mustard, peach preserves and lemon juice in a saucepan; heat until warm. Pour over the cooked chicken cubes and marinate (soak) for 1 hour.

Have an adult heat up the outdoor grill.

Thread chicken cubes onto skewers. Have an adult grill outside over medium heat for about 10 minutes, or until warmed throughout. Serve immediately.

Makes 8 servings. 176 calories, 2 fat grams per serving.

Potato Daggers

2 baking potatoes
seasoning salt
non-fat cooking spray
pepper

Preheat oven to 350 degrees F.

Line a sheet pan with foil.

Wash the potatoes. Cut the potato length-wise into eight slim wedges. Lay your potato daggers on a sheet pan. Lightly coat all the wedges with cooking spray.

Sprinkle with seasoning salt and a little pepper, to your taste.
Bake for 45 minutes.

From Chef Hilly

Makes 4 servings. 200 calories, less than 1 fat gram per serving.

Chicken Burgers

1 pound ground chicken breast
½ cup finely chopped carrots
½ cup finely chopped onion
½ cup breadcrumbs
1 egg
salt and pepper to taste
non-fat cooking spray
8 hamburger buns

In a bowl, mix ground chicken, carrots and onions together. Add egg, breadcrumbs, salt and pepper. Mush it all together really well! Make eight round patties from the mixture.

Preheat a large skillet on stove (for about three minutes on high), then coat skillet with cooking spray. Lower the stove temperature to medium high.

Place patties in skillet and cook on each side until brown and cooked throughout.

Makes 8 servings. 231 calories, 4 fat grams per serving.

Double Disk Salad

5 Roma tomatoes, sliced
1 large cucumber, sliced
2 tablespoons low-fat Italian dressing
lettuce leaves

Slice the tomatoes & cucumbers into thin disks. Clean the lettuce leaves, pat dry, and lay on a serving plate.

In the bowl, toss the tomatoes and the cucumbers with the dressing. Arrange on the lettuce leaves and serve!

Makes 2 servings. 68 calories, 2 fat grams per serving.

Build Your Own Nachos

1 package taco seasoning (you'll use 2 tablespoons)
½ cup fat-free sour cream
1 cup chopped lettuce
1 cup chopped tomatoes
1 cup shredded cooked chicken breast
¼ cup low-fat mozzarella cheese
1 bag of low-fat tortilla nacho chips (about 2 cups)

Blend 2 tablespoons of the taco seasoning with the sour cream together and set aside.

Put a layer of tortilla chips on a large plate. Top with shredded chicken, lettuce and tomatoes. Sprinkle cheese over top.

Microwave on high for 1-2 minutes, until cheese is melted. Remove from microwave and top with dollops of the spicy dip.

Makes 4 servings. 205 calories, 5 fat grams per serving.

Easy Chili Soup

1 pound ground turkey breast
1 medium onion, chopped
1 15-ounce can corn, drained
1 15-ounce can pinto beans
1 15-ounce can chopped tomatoes
1 15-ounce can spaghetti sauce
1 cup water
salt and pepper to taste

On the stove, cook turkey breast and onion in large pot on medium-high until brown. Drain off fat; add all other ingredients.

Bring to a simmer and cook for 30 minutes. Add a small amount of additional water if needed, and salt and pepper to taste.

Makes 8 servings. 192 calories, 2 fat grams per serving.

Hot Diggity Dog!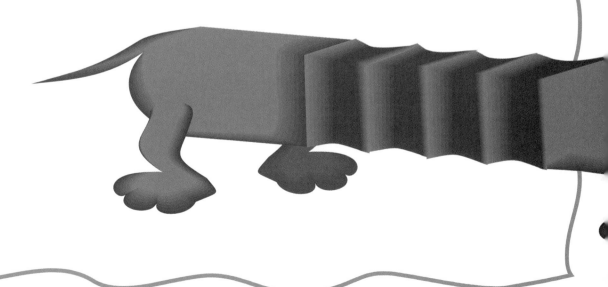

2 chicken or turkey hot dogs
2 hot dog buns
mustard
ketchup
2 large lettuce leaves

Boil or microwave the hot dogs until hot. Put each dog in a bun and decorate the hot dog with a face, using mustard for the eyes, ketchup for the mouth, and lettuce for the hair. Enjoy!

From Rylan B., age 8

Makes 2 servings. 273 calories, 7 fat grams per serving.

Sloppy Dogs

2 chicken or turkey hot dogs, sliced in ¼ inch rounds
1 15-ounce can pinto beans, drained
1 15-ounce can chili-style chunky tomatoes
¼ cup low-fat shredded mozzarella cheese
4 hamburger buns

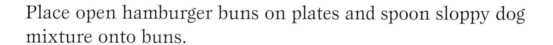

In a small microwave-safe bowl, combine hot dogs, pinto beans, and tomatoes.

Heat for two minutes on high. Have a grown-up remove the hot bowl from the microwave oven.

Place open hamburger buns on plates and spoon sloppy dog mixture onto buns.

Sprinkle with cheese and serve immediately.

Makes 4 servings. 329 calories, 6 fat grams per serving.

Frozen Fruit Cup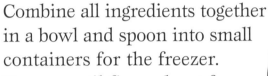

1 cup applesauce

1 10-ounce package frozen
    strawberries, thawed

1 11-ounce can mandarin oranges,
    drained

2 tablespoons orange juice
    concentrate

Combine all ingredients together
in a bowl and spoon into small
containers for the freezer.
Freeze until firm, about four
hours. Let sit at room temperature for 20 minutes
before serving.

Makes 6 servings. 95 calories, less than 1 fat gram per serving.

Strawberry Fruit Dip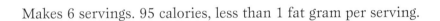

1 8-ounce container fat-free strawberry cream cheese

1 7-ounce jar marshmallow creme

1 pint strawberries, washed

Mix cream cheese and marshmallow creme together until
smooth. Serve with strawberries for dipping.

From Bren J., age 11

Makes 7 servings. 137 calories, less than 1 fat gram per serving.

30-Second Fruit Salad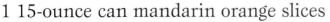

1 15-ounce can mandarin orange slices
1 banana, sliced
Maraschino cherries for garnish

Open can of oranges and pour out juice. Put oranges and banana slices in bowl and top with a few cherries.

Makes 2 servings. 153 calories, less than 1 fat gram per serving.

Yogurt Banana Pops

1 cup sliced ripe banana
⅓ cup low-fat vanilla yogurt
½ cup 2% milk

aluminum foil and popsicle mold
wooden popsicle sticks

In a bowl, mash the bananas well with a fork. Add yogurt and milk and mix well.

Pour into popsicle molds or small cups and cover tightly with foil. Take a popsicle stick and poke one through the foil in the center of each pop. Place in freezer overnight.

Secret Tip!

Use FOIL or PLASTIC WRAP to hold your sticks in place when you freeze your pops. Your sticks will always come out sticking straight up!

Makes 4 servings. 58 calories, 1 fat gram per serving.

Orange Juice Pops 🍳🍳

1 64-ounce container of fresh orange juice

plastic wrap and popsicle mold
wooden popsicle sticks

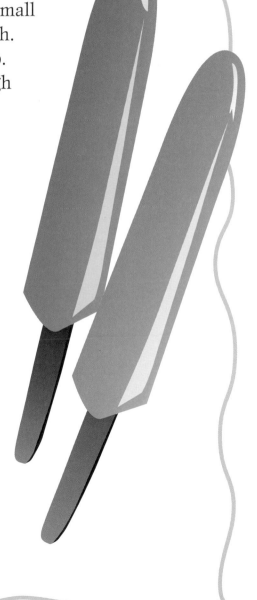

Pour orange juice into popsicle molds or small cups, leaving ½ inch of space at top of each. Cover containers tightly with plastic wrap. Take a popsicle stick and poke one through the plastic wrap in the center of each pop. Place in freezer for 4-6 hours.

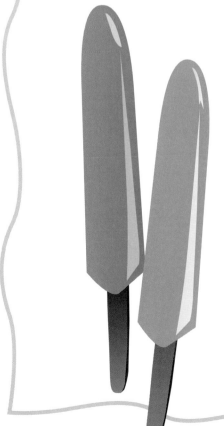

Makes 16 servings. 56 calories, less than 1 fat gram per serving.

Tornado Swirls

1 cup cake flour, sifted
¾ teaspoon baking powder
¼ teaspoon salt
4 large eggs
1 cup sugar
1 teaspoon vanilla extract
2 tablespoons water
1 cup strawberry preserves (no added sugar)
½ cup chopped strawberries

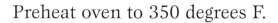

Preheat oven to 350 degrees F.

Line 13" x 17" half-sheet pan with foil (overhang by 2"). Grease the foil and dust with flour.

Sift flour, baking powder and salt together and set aside. Whip together eggs and sugar; add vanilla toward the end. When fluffy, fold in half of the dry ingredients and the water, just until blended. DO NOT OVER MIX! Gently fold in the remaining dry ingredients. Pour batter into pan and spread evenly. Bake for 10-12 minutes.

When the cake is done, remove from oven; place another foil-lined sheet pan on top of the cake and flip over. Remove pans.

To remove the foil without tearing the cake, start at one end and gently roll the foil back to the other end. Let stand for about 10 minutes.

Mix strawberry preserves with chopped strawberries and pour, then spread, over the top of the cake.

Roll the cake lengthwise until you reach the end.

Magnifique!

Makes 6 servings. 312 calories, 4 fat grams per serving.

Worms in the Mud

2 small packages low-fat chocolate pudding mix
3 ½ cups 2% milk
1 tub reduced-fat frozen whipped topping
10 reduced-fat Oreo® cookies, crushed
bag of gummy worms (approx. 21 pieces)

8 small clear plastic cups

Prepare pudding mix according to directions, using low-fat milk. Fold in whipped topping.

Fill each cup about a quarter of the way with pudding mixture.

Add some crushed cookies and gummy worms, more pudding and end with crushed cookies to look like dirt. Refrigerate for at least one hour before serving.

Makes 8 servings. 302 calories, 5 fat grams per serving.

Edible Card for that Special Occasion!

2 graham crackers
1 container low-fat chocolate pudding
1 container low-fat vanilla pudding
colored sprinkles

cookie sheet (one that fits in the freezer!)

Spread ½ cup chocolate pudding on one graham cracker. Lightly place another graham cracker on top and place on your cookie sheet. Spread vanilla pudding evenly over top cracker. Put this in the freezer for 30 minutes.

Place the remaining chocolate pudding in a plastic squeeze bottle (an empty plastic ketchup container works well!). Write your words and make designs on the frozen "card." Add sprinkles for color.

Freeze for another 30 minutes before delivering.

From Kyh D., age 7

Makes 1 serving. 266 calories, 5 fat grams per serving.

Chocolate Banana Bars

3 bananas
2 chocolate bars (about 1.5 ounces each)
1 tablespoon granola
1 tablespoon crispy rice cereal

6 wooden popsicle sticks
wax paper

Peel bananas and cut each in half in the middle. Push a popsicle stick through the flat, cut part of the banana and lay on plate. Cover with plastic wrap and freeze in the freezer for about 2 hours.

Microwave the candy bars on high for about 2 minutes or until melted. Stir in the cereal and granola.

Cover a plate with wax paper. Spread the mixture evenly around the six banana bars.

Place the bars on wax paper and cover with another sheet of wax paper. Freeze for another hour before serving.

Makes 6 servings. 135 calories, 4 fat grams per serving.

Fish in the Water

2 boxes blueberry Jell-O® gelatin
1 can fruit cocktail, drained well
gummy fish
small glass goldfish bowl

Make Jell-O® according to package directions.

Put drained fruit cocktail in the bottom of the goldfish bowl and pour Jell-O® slowly on top. Place in refrigerator to set.

When Jell-O® is starting to thicken, remove the bowl from the refrigerator and add gummy fish; arrange them in the "water" above the fruit cocktail.

Put back in refrigerator and allow Jell-O® to set completely.

From Kyh D., age 7

Party size!

Makes 8 servings. 150 calories, 1 fat gram per serving.

No-Bake Boulders

½ cup reduced-fat
    smooth peanut butter
½ cup honey
½ cup low-fat granola
½ cup crispy rice cereal
½ cup raisins
½ cup crushed graham crackers

wax paper

Heat peanut butter and honey in
a pan over low heat until creamy.
Remove from heat and pour
into a bowl to cool.

Add granola, cereal, raisins and
graham cracker crumbs to the
peanut butter mix, and stir it
all together.

"Now don't go
and eat it right
from the bowl!"

Roll into balls and set on wax paper.
Refrigerate at least one hour before eating.

Makes 12 servings. 155 calories, 5 fat grams per serving.

Blueprints to Build!

Build your own food creations using our "blueprints" on the following pages as your guides. Be creative and experiment with new designs and different ingredients. Let your imagination be your guide!

Parents — these "blueprints" are great for rainy-day activities, school projects, and parties!

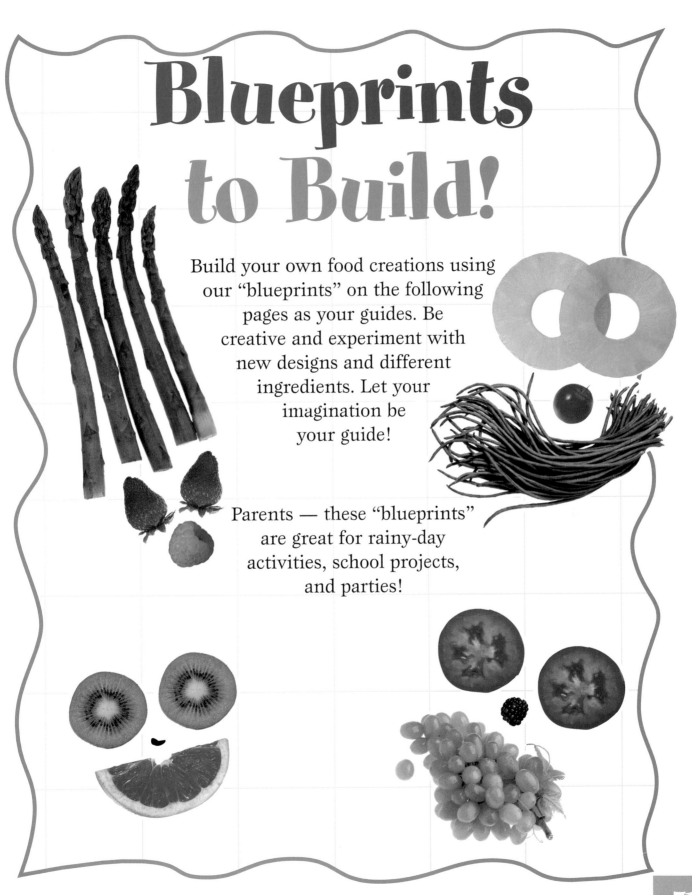

Alien Encounters

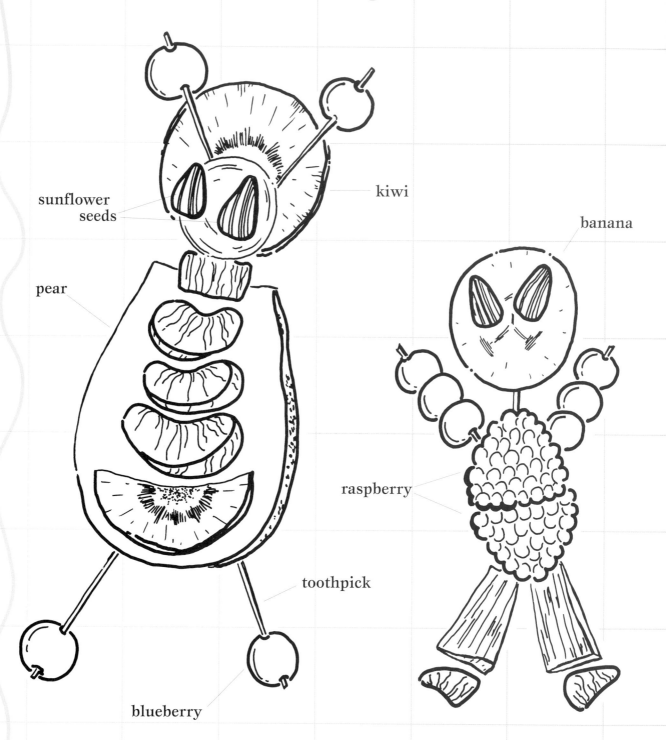

sunflower seeds

kiwi

banana

pear

raspberry

toothpick

blueberry

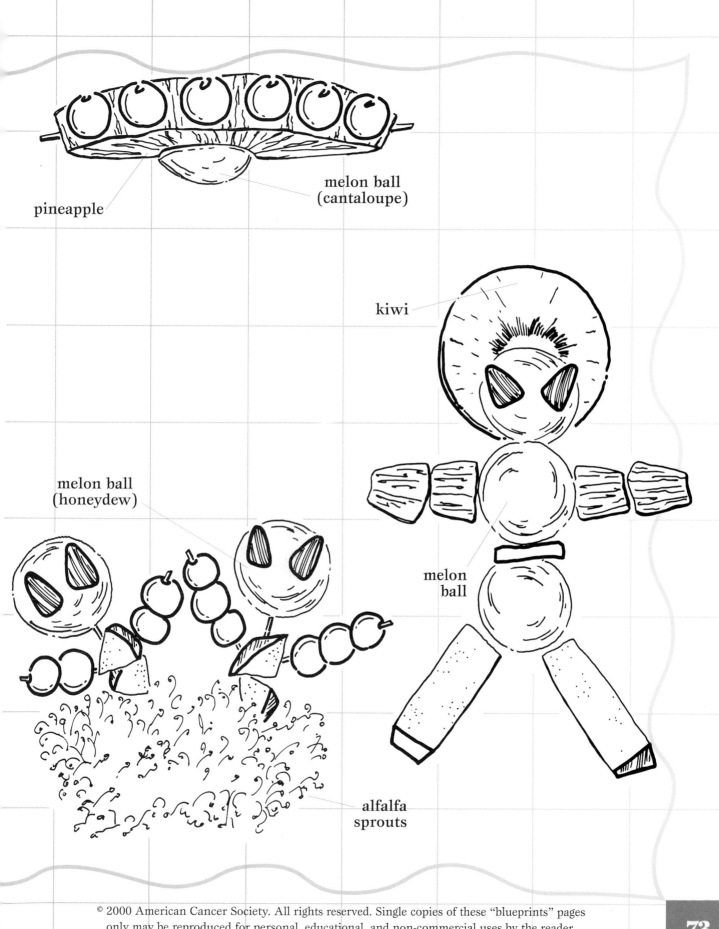

pineapple

melon ball
(cantaloupe)

kiwi

melon ball
(honeydew)

melon
ball

alfalfa
sprouts

Funny Faces

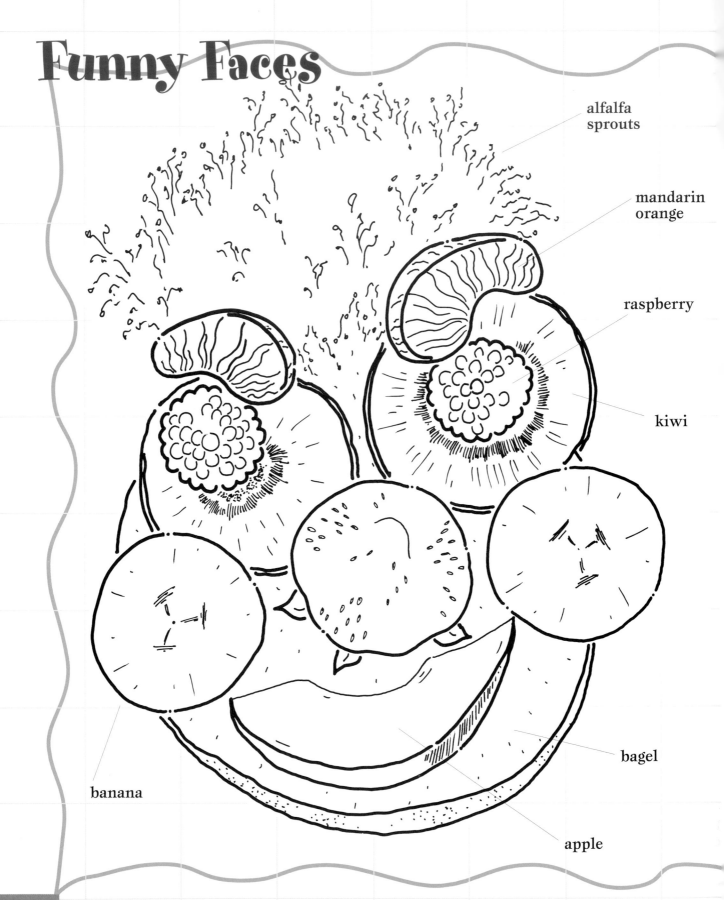

alfalfa
sprouts

mandarin
orange

raspberry

kiwi

banana

bagel

apple

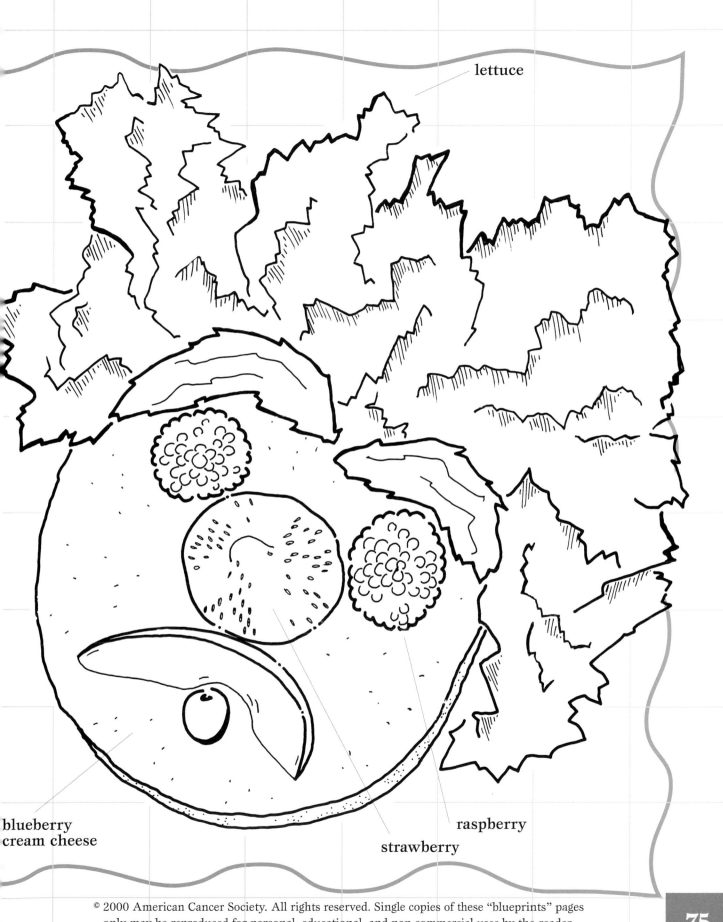

lettuce

blueberry
cream cheese

raspberry

strawberry

Flower Power

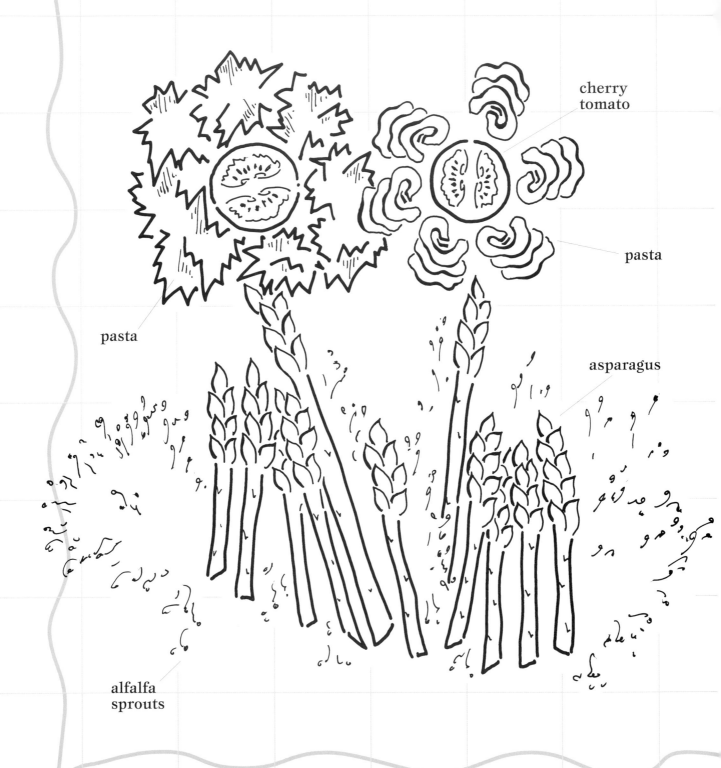

cherry tomato

pasta

pasta

asparagus

alfalfa sprouts

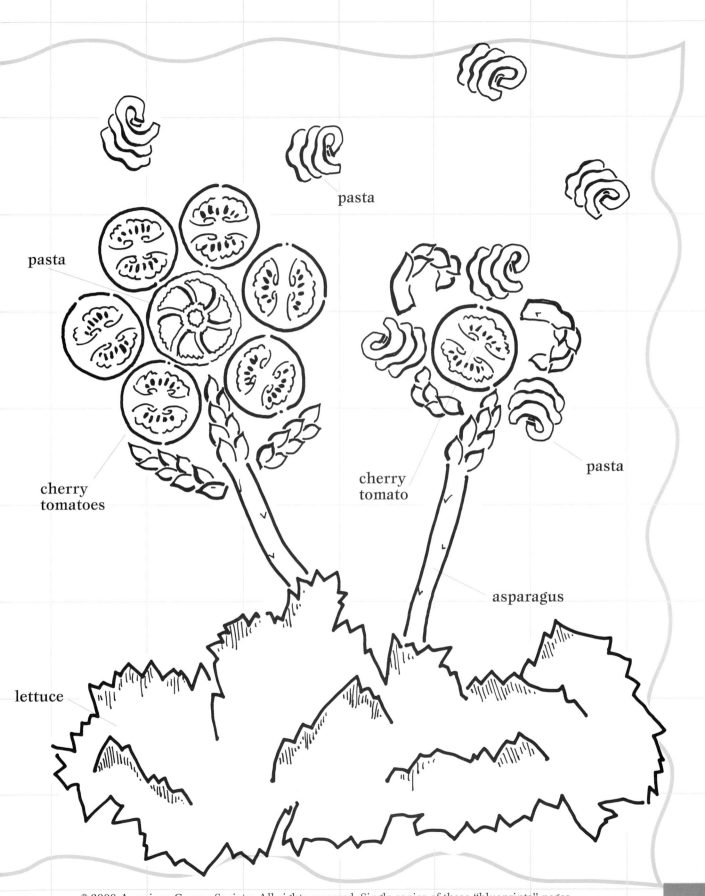

pasta

pasta

cherry
tomatoes

cherry
tomato

pasta

asparagus

lettuce

77

Dinosaur Hunter

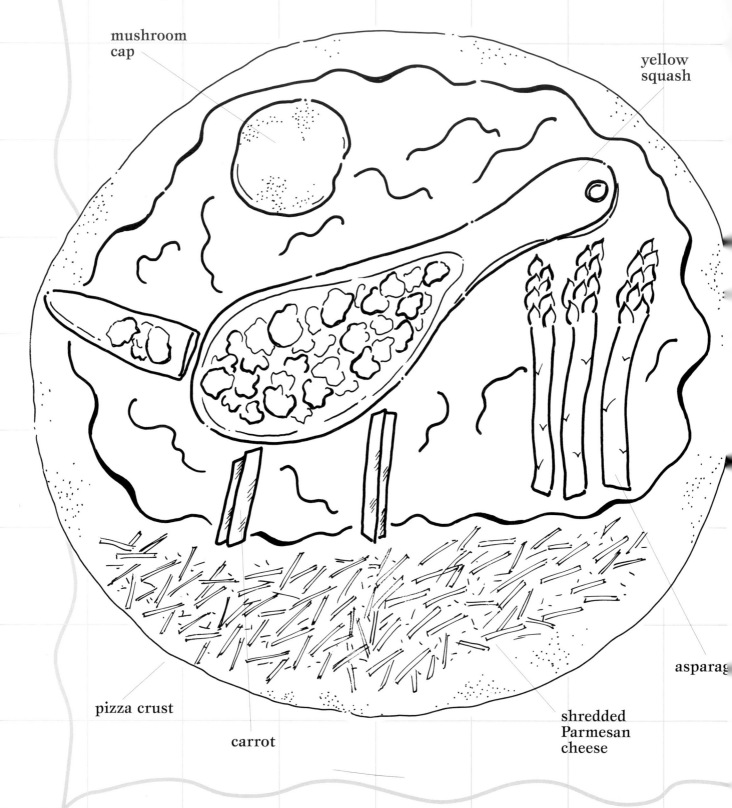

mushroom cap

yellow squash

pizza crust

carrot

shredded Parmesan cheese

asparag

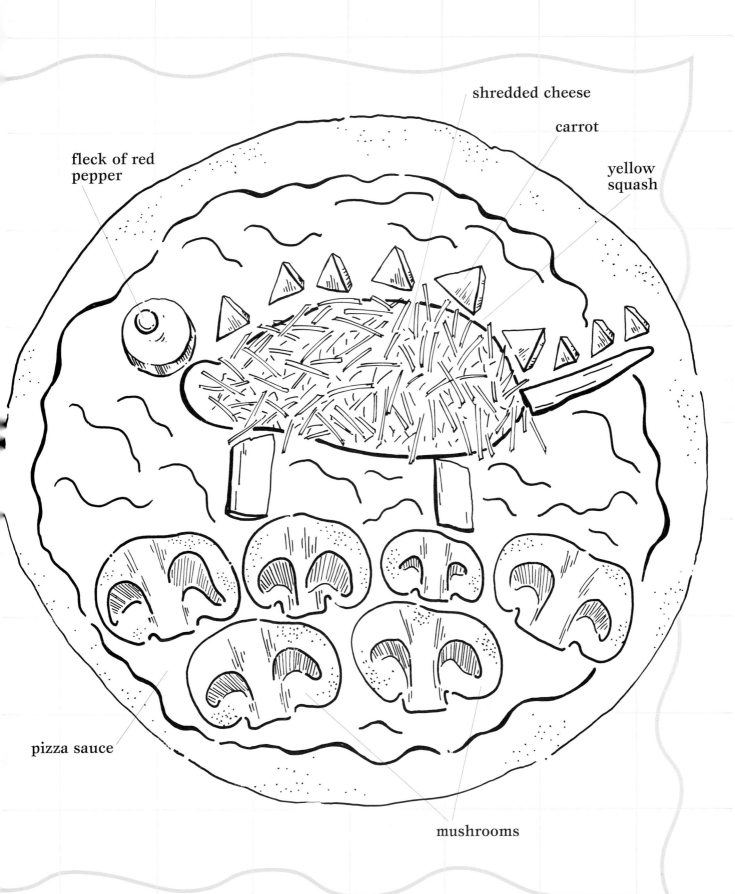

fleck of red pepper

shredded cheese

carrot

yellow squash

pizza sauce

mushrooms

Home Improvements

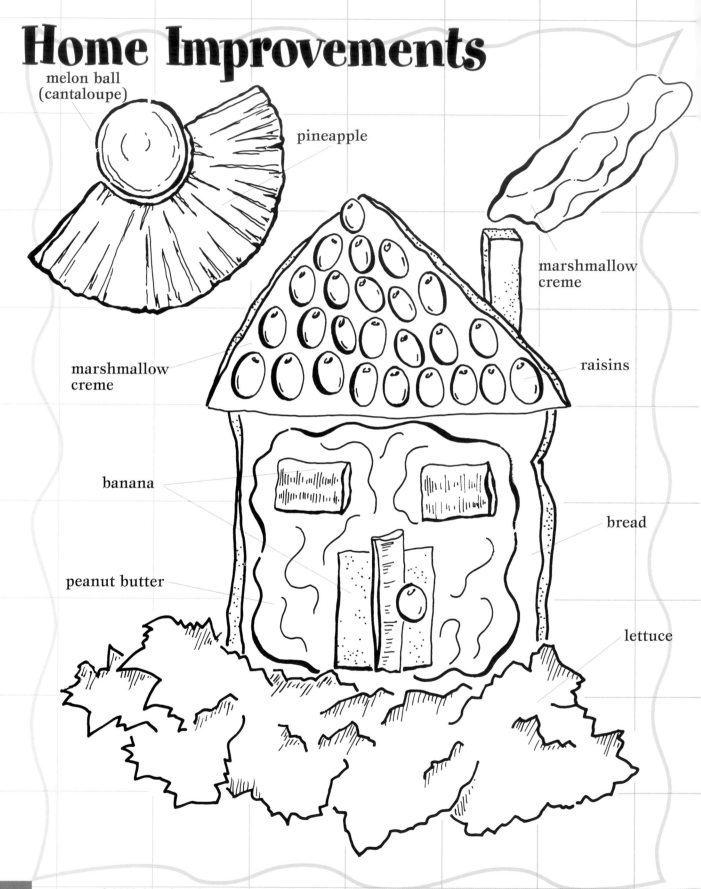

melon ball
(cantaloupe)

pineapple

marshmallow
creme

marshmallow
creme

raisins

banana

bread

peanut butter

lettuce

Parents' Section

Reducing Fats in Recipes

Eating out with the Family

Reducing Fats in Recipes

Sometimes you can substitute one food ingredient for another and end up with a healthier dish that tastes just as good as the original. Here are some good rules of thumb:

Substitutions to baked goods may result in differences in flavor as well as texture. Each recipe is different, so you may need to experiment to get it right.

Light butter should not be used for baking, since its moisture content is different from that of butter or regular margarine.

In general, change one ingredient in a recipe at a time. (Casseroles and soups can easily be changed, but jellies and candy recipes should not be altered.)

To keep your lowfat baked goods moist, bake at a slightly lower temperature:

cakes, muffins, quick breads	350° Fahrenheit
biscuits and scones	375° Fahrenheit
brownies	325° Fahrenheit
cookies	275°-300° Fahrenheit

Once you're ready to get started, try these substitutions:

❦ In recipes that call for oil as the only liquid, try a combination of half applesauce and half buttermilk.

❦ Pureéd prunes or baby food prunes are a good fat replacement in baked chocolate goodies such as brownies and cakes. They add naturally sweet flavor and chewy texture.

❦ Substitute 2 egg whites per egg in baked goods.

❦ When recipes call for chocolate chips, try ½ chocolate chips and ½ raisins. When recipes call for nuts, use half the amount and toast them in the oven first. This brings out more flavor in the nuts. Or try substituting raisins or browned rolled oats instead.

❦ In place of regular cottage cheese, try low-fat or fat-free cottage cheese. In place of regular cream cheese, try light cream cheese or Neufchatel cheese.

❦ Many recipes that call for ground beef (lasagna, meat balls, burgers) can be replaced with ground turkey breast instead. Be sure to use turkey **breast** though, as ground turkey contains the skin and can have as high a fat content as beef.

❦ Use evaporated skim milk instead of heavy cream in sauces and soups.

❦ Whipped cream can be replaced with non-fat whipped topping in most recipes.

Eating out with the Family

Kids love to eat out, but are they always ordering the same burger and fries? Here are some great tips for eating out *and* eating well:

- **Take** an apple with you to the restaurant and slice it while the kids are waiting for their food to arrive.

- **Order** an appetizer with vegetables or fruit in it, or have your server bring the salads first.

- **Experiment with** some new dish that you've never tried before. Perhaps the grilled fish or a new vegetable dish. Have everyone try the dish and comment on it.

- **Play** the Food Guide Pyramid game! Try to identify the foods and where they come from. See how the meals fit with the pyramid recommendations.

- **Introduce** the salad bar. Kids will love the selection and the opportunity to try new vegetables with dip or low fat salad dressing.

- **Try** rice as a side dish instead of the French fries on the kids' menu, or ask the restaurant if they have any of your kids' favorite vegetables to substitute.

- **Choose** one healthier regular menu item and split it between two kids, instead of ordering the kids menu items, which can often be fried. Have it be a treat for them to order from the "big" menu. Your cost will often be the same or less.

- **Ask** the restaurant if they have low-fat substitutes for items such as sour cream, cream cheese, salad dressing or mayonnaise. Order foods grilled instead of fried, and if the dish has a creamy sauce, ask for it on the side.

- **Order** reduced fat milk instead of whole milk.

- **Set** a good example for younger kids. Many times they want to eat what an older sibling or parent is eating.

- **Play** games with the younger ones. Broccoli can be trees, cauliflower can be snow-covered trees. Kids can pretend to be their favorite plant-eating dinosaur and devour their veggies.

Index

Index

Index

Index

Contributors

BILLY HOWARD

Hilly Blondheim

Chef Hilly specializes in children's cooking programs, working in print, multimedia and television. Shortly after graduation, he started a successful children's after-school cooking program in Atlanta, engaging hundreds of children in the joy of cooking. He credits his success to his wonderful family, and all the teachers who took time to help him, especially Linda Taffet, DeeDee Schols and Norm Herrick. He is a graduate of the School of Culinary Arts in Atlanta.

Billy Howard

Billy is a commercial and documentary photographer with an emphasis on health, education and social themes. His work has been exhibited internationally and is in the permanent collections of the Library of Congress, the High Museum of Art and the Carter Presidential Center. He was an artist-in-residence at the National School of Photography in France and has received numerous grants for his works. He received an Honorary Doctor of Literature Degree from St. Andrews College in 1996.

MARILYN SURIANI

Pam Drake

Pam is a commercial and fine art photographer with a BFA in photography from Georgia State University. In addition to her photography career, where she shoots weddings, plays, schools and cemeteries, she has taught sailing, pedaled her bicycle around the state of Georgia and cooked up some mighty fine dishes.